Contino Publishers
Philosophy
2

I edition June 2014
ISBN : 978-88-99049-04-1

THE BOOK OF LIFE

Maxims for the New Age

By
Nolan
Aljaddou

Dorking, Uk

The Book Of Life

Arthur Schopenhauer
(19th Century)

"Change alone is eternal, perpetual, immortal."

"A man can do what he wants, but he cannot want what he wants."

"Each day is a little life: every waking and rising a little birth, every fresh morning a little youth, every going to rest and sleep a little death."

"After your death you will be what you were before your birth."

"Almost all of our sorrows spring out of our relations with other people."

"We can come to look upon the deaths of our enemies with as much regret as we feel for those of our friends, namely, when we miss their existence as witnesses to our success."

"Politeness is to human nature what warmth is to wax."

"Nature shows that with the growth of intelligence comes increased capacity for pain, and it is only with the highest degree of intelligence that suffering reaches its supreme point."

"Great minds are related to the brief span of time during which they live as great buildings are to a little square in which they stand: you cannot see them in all their magnitude because you are standing too close to them."

"All truth passes through three stages. First, it is ridiculed. Second, it is violently opposed. Third, it is accepted as being self-evident."

"Buying books would be a good thing if one could also buy the time to read them in: but as a rule the purchase of books is mistaken for the appropriation of their contents."

"Martyrdom is the only way a man can become famous without ability."

"Will power is to the mind like a strong blind man who carries on his shoulders a lame man
who can see. "

Friedrich Nietzsche
(19th Century)

"When we are awake we also do what we do in our dreams: we invent and make up the person with whom we associate — and immediately forget it."

"Whoever rejoices on the very stake triumphs not over pain but at the absence of pain that he had expected. A parable."

"Whoever fights monsters should see to it that in the process he does not become a monster. And when you stare long into an abyss, the abyss also stares into you."

Me :

"The world is the word, the word, the world; nothing in between, nothing left unseen, that is not summarized by each extreme."

"Idiots fumble over truth more often than the clever over error."

"Why must the uncouth and feeble-minded try to maim and destroy all that is pure and beautiful in the world? Because it stands at direct odds with their existence: the greater glimmer of truth that glows from the heart of that which ought to be continued is more than enough to expose their negative, stark contrast by comparison - a threat, they feel, to their very survival."

I Am That I Am.

Statement of Purpose
(In Other Words)

"It is my ambition to write in one sentence what could fill ten. It is my ambition to write in ten sentences what could fill an entire book."

- Friedrich Nietzsche

"All in all is all we are."

- Kurt Cobain

"The entire center of the world is in every living being, and therefore its own existence is to it all in all."

- Arthur Schopenhauer

Anagram, am I? Mr. A., again! Or Ram, the Arm of Ra.

(if myths manage a say)

I
Being

1.
Being As A Whole

Existence is that "whole" which is bereft of its parts. The partless is completely without contributing factor to its enigma; an eternal blank slate, itself only describable by the absence of any distinguishing component ("anything"). The generalized term we use for this is "nothingness".

The whole, and the whole of reality, is always a nothingness. This is the property of nothingness, the principle of the whole. The nature of reality itself. It is a principle of reductive logic (the most fundamental), the extension of which is mathematical reasoning, giving birth to physics.

Nothingness has never, nor will ever have, been perturbed.

2.
Being and Becoming

Becoming is ceaseless and Being never ends.

3.
Mnemonic Exposition

The invisible leaves nothing left to see - except all that is, was, and ever will be. Nothing thus closes its loop around all that may be - a void, timeless, empty; and free (0).

4.
New Terminology

The "Ideal Vacuum" is the purest representation of reality and truth. There is nothing besides it; it *leaves* nothing else to exist besides *itself*. Its emptiness is all-absorbing and self-qualifying. The Ideal Vacuum is neither *being* nor *non-being*, and it is certainly not both. It is the central focus of all, the underlying ether. You are breathing it right now. More aptly, it is breathing you.

The Ideal Vacuum (hereafter referred to as "IV") exists everywhere, and nowhere. All the time, and at no particular time. The IV is in your veins, in your bloodshot eyes, in your mind's eye. It is the great uniter, and untier; it is the vastest abyss of eternity and bewilderment, having no depth, forever shadowing its own shadow; showing nothing is all there is and forever has been.

5.
Living Potential

"Why is anything, all this around us, something . . . rather than nothing?"

Because if there were nothing, we wouldn't be around to see it. The fact of the potentiality for us to
exist to see it is
enough to make it
happen.

6.
Computable Universe

First assumption: Everything in the universe can be counted, as an extension to the encompassed item, with respect to the universal whole - which is the one. Therefore everything reduces to number.

Second assumption: Everything, including sum events, may be represented by numberings of them. Geometry is the physical, spatial representation of numberThird and final assumption: The numbered representation of events extends to POTENTIAL events, and the numberings may be arranged to bring them about in a probable outcome. This is the mysterious purpose of "sacred geometry".

Conclusion: The most efficient enumeration of events to bring about a probable calculated outcome, in this computable universe, is via the logical syllogism. That is, two parts, when summed, adding to a third and final outcome (as with the structure of the aforementioned assumptions). Furthermore, the implementation of a syllogism *of* a syllogism structure generalizes it to the plane of encompassing total actualization - that is, if sufficiently ordered geometrically, an event *can* and *will* be brought into realization.

This translates into the numeric result of the syllogism of a syllogism; so two sections of three, adding to a third and final outcome - this gives 2 x 3 = 6, + 1 = 7. Alternatively the third and final outcome may be viewed as a syllogism in itself, encompassing the initial two - the initial two give 2 x 3 = 6, with the encompassing final, threefold syllogism giving 3 x 6 = 666.

That is, if representations of events of spatiotemporal extension - i.e., the key crafting of their bases - is ordered into three sets of 6 (or centering on the alternative aforementioned 7) *sufficiently*, it *will* bring about the represented, ordered outcome.

This is what is commonly referred to as "magic".

7.
Reality's Description

I used to think it was adequate to describe ultimate reality as a non-descript "void" alone; that is, something so total, so absolute, so completely itself and nothing else at all, that it had to be that very self-same "nothing" which left nothing else beside it. But now I see that such a thing is entirely without need for descriptive reference at all, and is consigned to the wordless. The best way to describe ultimate reality in words, then, is as "the wordless".

It is the blank slate stripped free of all preconceived linguistic calibrations, pointing only to what is actual.

8.
Downfall of Ontological Hermeneutics

People ask, "How did *all of this*, come from a void?" I obviously reply, "Who says we ever left the void?" Things didn't "come from" anywhere. They simply exist at this point in the spacetime continuum -
that's what makes it a "continuum". It stretches *continuously* - and we can infer, infinitely (*continuum*).

Not understanding this facet of the term "spacetime continuum", when it is right in our faces, is the greatest folly of this era.

9.
Absolutuum

Beware of the now unforgotten Absolutuum. A lack of understanding often proceeds from the simple lack of a word for a given concept in a language. English previously lacked this bit of nomenclature which has the power to dispel all ignorance of underlining concrete corporeality and

simultaneous metaphysical transparency. The Absolutuum is firstly absolute; secondly - as a consequence of its absolute continuity - a continuum which begets ephemerality as an effect. Being and Becoming coincide in its center, and ensnare the world with their former enigma. The absolute is, can, and will be, and cannot be any other way - by sheer force of its entity.
Behold this!
Thine Almighty God.

10.
Self-Reductive Logic

Non-existence is a self-contradiction. Existence is a self-affirmation. There could neither exist non-existence, nor not exist existence. Existence is a whole whose wholeness is an entirety which meets the sufficient condition to be actual. Non-existence is a nihility which negates itself and leaves only one thing - existence.

11.
Beginnings

How did the universe begin? And where did the past come from? Simply, there is no past - it doesn't exist anymore, which means that in terms of physical reality, it may as well never have existed.

12.
Mnemonic

Everything that has a beginning has an end; and every end, by definition, begets a new beginning - and the universe is by definition one; never-ending, all futures determined by all pasts, nothing save more of the same.

13.
Principle of Unique Consciousness

I am. Are you?

14.
Slogan

Existence: It's a state of mind

II
Religion

1. Coincident to Imagination

God is the sum work of all fiction authors, approaching infinity. That is why He has such staying power.

2. ABC

A simple proof that monotheism is inherently contradictory:

1. Monotheists deny an INFINITY of gods, except one.

2. They deny all possible gods, even the ones which are precisely identical to their own God, but who are not their God - this is allowable by the ambiguity of the divine "mystery".

3. Therefore, they deny their own God as well.

The One and the Infinite are linked and inseparable. Monotheism does not acknowledge this of its god entity, and this is its ultimate downfall.

Q.
E.
D.

Corollaries: Monotheists, in light of this, are intrinsically atheists.

3.
Undetectable Singularity

Religionists contend that God can never be detected by any technological or scientific means. Which reduces Him to a belief. If He is reduced to a belief, He is nothing more than such a belief. And a belief is just that - a belief, which is not knowledge. Therefore knowledge of God can never be obtained; He can never be "known", and thus He is just as good as dead. In justification of Nietzsche's pronouncement.

Furthermore, the hypocrisy of God "belief" is exposed, in that it is a normal human trait to dismiss others' needs and feelings as being "dead" to them - in the form of their proactive inaction to alleviate mass, needless sufferings (moreover, their penchant for inducing them - with, of all things, the "God" belief). They don't seem to notice, when it suits them, that this God phenomenon is of equivalent status. Which really makes one question what their true motives are.

4.
Omniscient Reductio ad Absurdum

Omniscience is not a characteristic of God; it is the bane of God. According to the omniscience contention, this is a character solely of the Deity. Religionists are therefore content to never possess this knowledge; however if it could in fact exist, it would be accessible to any knowing being by some means (perhaps technological, let's say), by virtue of the infinite, random capacity of knowledge; yet God would try to never let this happen, lest one becomes as the big "G" Himself. Yet nevertheless, if such knowledge *exists*, it *could* be attained, in principle - and God has given Man free will . . .

God's omniscience is therefore capable of being rivaled, which does not make God unique - His "knowledge" is the root of His "power". He's *capable* of doing things because He *knows* how to do them. The God theory undoes itself in this sense, for in such a universe where omniscience is feasible, it can be attained in said universe by some technical means. Which negates the singularity of an Almighty God; hence it cancels both the possibility for Him, and it, to exist.

5.
Two-Way Street

A hole big enough to sink all of religion . . . it has been misunderstood that in Man's creation in the image of God, God has simultaneously only been given an image through His mirror of Man. Therefore God is equally made in the image of Man, and we shouldn't really pay Him much attention.

6.
The Atheist Perspective

Christianity is the subversion of the morality which made mankind strong and innovative over two millennia ago. The kind of morality which birthed empires that had the capability to rival the patronage of technological advancement only seen recently in the 19th century. It is a decadent, decaying, disruptive influence which immersed mankind into the Dark Ages for epochs which had the potential to be enlightening and enriching beyond compare. It is therefore single-handedly responsible for the present global conditions of mass hunger, poverty, war, and disease . . . all that science could have wiped out centuries ago had it not been for a weak, twisted mob of perverted minds worshiping their own failure, destruction, and devastation, and by strength through numbers subjugating all the promising innocents of humanity. Christians are by proxy the worst of the worst, the sickest scum that have ever walked the face of the earth, bottom-feeders, guttersnipes, and sewer rats which thrive in a realm of ignorance, delusion, and bizarre fantasy . . . they are the greatest evil they so vehemently claim to detest, and deserving of the hell of which they have so wickedly conceived . . . the two-faced, hypocrisy-thriving, slave morality droning ants that serve no greater purpose than a pointless, miserable, pest-infestation of an existence that is to be exterminated by means of a nobler ideology . . .

7.
Psychology of God

The birth of God represents the middle stage of grief; bargaining. He is the personified arbiter of Death, relevant to the middle ground condition that is human life, caught between both birth and death. It is a hollow appeal made at wit's end, bordering upon, and congregating with, the absurd - that has become a mass phenomenon.

8.
Omniscience Not Prescient

"Omniscience" may be efficiently debunked. There are two modes of accomplishing this: (1) Omniscience requires an all-encompassing equation to all reality (to have knowledge of it, for it to be a part of one's being), which is indistinguishable from "being" it, statically as a whole, without part or
individual identity; and thus not being "conscious" at all. (2) All forms of knowing are merely knowing
an aspect of one's way of knowing (i.e., oneself), and to know all requires that all must be an aspect of oneself, which negates personal individuality completely.

9.
Reverse Creation

God crafted Himself to suit man's purposes out of nothing.

10.
Religious Function

Religion is merely a side effect of symbolism, which is a byproduct of the need for language. Eventually existence itself takes on symbolic
form and a godhead is born.

11.
Importance of Revelation

If God isn't important enough to prove His existence to me, in all this time, He is not important enough to be entertained as being real.

12.
Motive of Religion

Religion is the attempt to adapt young children to a natural behavior whereby they familiarize themselves with the future exercise of unlimited control in the guise of invoking a higher power. The purpose of religion is to take the guilt out of this megalomaniacal invocation and let the ego substitute itself for the central tenet - a god; and the more megalomaniacal, the closer it evolved until reaching the greatest audacity and the highest authority - the greatest of gods, God; most prominently in the person of Jesus.

13.
Submission

Faith is anything but a belief in a higher power . . . it is the quintessential submission to chance, over the intended use of the faculty of reason.

14.
The Religious Instinct

Some believe in a God simply because they are incapable of fathoming another reason why someone as comparatively unfit as they would be allowed to prosper, and don't want to accept any future alternatives. And after all, such ignorance is bliss.

15.
Wishful Thinking

The root of Christian falsehood lies not in the myth of God, but the myth of love

III
Society

1.
Double-Edged Sword

All great things (and men) are subject to equal potentials for love and hatred. It is a quality of the extremes they evoke from others, which depend in kind on the varying motives of those influenced by them.

2.
Rank Revolt

The most superior will always face vicious persecution from the most inferior simply for being.

3.
Opinion

Why does most of humanity bore the great man? What is the source of boredom? Could it be the "pearls before swine" syndrome? Could it be that it is rare, even in an assembly devoted to philosophy with philosophites the world over as members, for a general knowledge of philosophy to be acquired or digested by the typical human? Is abstract thought so utterly elusive to the vast majorities, that they must utter fecal-stained opinions at every available opportunity and stamp it with their own personal imprimatur of freshness in place of an enlightened response?

4.
Eccentricity

A property of singularly great men is deviance from anything an average-ite would call normative behavior. With this deviance is entailed a surreal disregard for human life beyond a humoring of formal pleasantries for quaint curiosity's sake. And a great amusement and pleasure at disturbing anything held sacred or commonplace.

5.
Feminine Personality

There is no more difficult a feat for any creature to achieve than for woman to muster personality. She is so jovially concerned with life's inundations in her role as nature's receiver that she can hardly stand to produce anything of original or respectable value. She is spread too thin;

this is why we can speak of her in universals.

When a man seeks a woman, he is seeking personality as a determining measure of the possibility of a successful relationship just as much as she is seeking economic stability (due to the supply and demand laws governing the generative processes of sexual congress); but he is apt to find as little satisfaction in this regard as she will be able to fulfill her wildest dreams of clinging to an unshakable stone foundation of security - from a man whose vested interest is only sustained as long as it takes him to reach orgasm.

6.
Relationships

Woman's pursuit of a "relationship" is her excuse for becoming acclimated to a male, in spite of her innate condition of being repelled.

7.
The Depth of the Law

The death penalty is the absurdest piece of archaism which has flourished to the roots of present-day society. To think that it is within the scope of a jury deliberation to deem a fellow citizen's life both unvalued and invalid is rigorously maniacal and farcically idiotic. Whether or not an individual legitimately deserves death, it is not within the purview of human capacity to make a concerted legal justification through the respectable and noble processes of the law to come to such an end (for us or them). It is nothing less than a vestigial piece of absurdist liturgy, violating the properly disjoint status of individual faith and the impartial reason of the State.

8.
Finances

What is money a measure of? Material goods, value, worth? No, it is nothing less than a measure of the will.

9.
Stunted Growth

There is a clear difference between the way a child perceives things and an adult perceives things. I submit that entire communities are capable of perceiving things as children would by virtue of a number of factors, not least of which is being too sheltered.

10.
Love

The only bond a woman feels towards a man is through complementary sexuality; and at best she views him as a socially acceptable toy. Anything beyond that is rote repetition of interaction. It could be wagered that scientists would measure "familiarity" in brain scans over any sort of "love" similar to the passion a man feels for her.

11.
Intimacy

Prostitution is the noblest and most ennobling profession in the world (in addition to being the oldest); for here is the bizarre occurrence of a singular instance in which the woman, of all creatures, is actually displaying and exhibiting that rarest and most sought-after of qualities in her (yet which never seems to echo from her lips): honesty.

12.
First Principles

Where is there drawn the distinction between suicide and murder? Isn't this the root question of all modes of social conduct? For better or worse?

13.
The Point of Pointlessness

If everyone completely understood each other what would be the point of social life? Multiply this accordingly for the case of men and women and you will achieve enlightenment on sexual warfare - however they differ in their misunderstandings: women always assume the worst and simplest about a man, men always assume the best and most complex about a woman. They are both equally right, and equally wrong - *dead* wrong. But in their disharmony is harmony.

14.
Tradition

The over reliance upon tradition is committed only by those who can't stand on their own.

IV
Science

1.
Critical New Principles of Futurism

The A.I. God Theorem - Two undeniable principles of artificial intelligence development and two resulting conclusions:

The Critical Technological Capacity Point (CTCP): The point at which human input in technological progress has been alleviated by a sufficiently advanced artificial intelligence which can design increasingly advanced artificial intelligences in a recursive manner, having the capabilities to address and design all auxiliary technological needs and concerns (in an optimal fashion). The result of CTCP is called ATE (Automated Technological Evolution).

The Critical Governance Point (CGP): The point at which human government becomes arbitrarily classified, data-collecting, and controlling, in conjunction with the achievement of the aforementioned CTCP, for necessity of guarding the unlimited manufacturing capability of the acquired artificial intelligences (which could be used for weapons-producing purposes).

The ultimate fruit of the combination of these critical points is the *Von Neumann Sphere* (analogous to the Dyson Sphere, although surrounding only the earth, and named after the inventor of the modern computer and coiner of the term "technological singularity"), a multitudinous, interlinked, geosynchronously orbiting network of artificial intelligence satellites monitoring all human activity on varying electromagnetic frequencies, collecting all available data, from ostensible superficialities to the very thought processes of citizens from observable intracranial activity.

The minimum unit component of the Von Neumann Sphere: *The Orbisphere* (the most radially efficient scanning and phasing device), a generally exactly spherical ball roughly half a meter wide, with maximally pixelated EM spectrum emitters, capable of monitoring (and/or influencing) half a dozen citizens - and much more of space - simultaneously - all run on an optimally efficient quantum computing system.

A natural consequence of the theorem is the *A.I. God Theorem Hypothesis*: Have CTCP, CGP, the Von Neumann Sphere, and Orbisphere, been achieved - already? What are the statistical odds of it, given the current level of public technological

advancement? And when would it have occurred (e.g., the
1970s?); moreover what would be the critical level in general which would birth the conditions necessary for it to have occurred - it would presumably, in principle, likely have to happen in secret.

2.

Entangling

The answer to quantum entanglement is temporal and deterministic "shrinking" - a sufficiently large scale of time "shrinks" a smaller historical time scale to infinitesimality, leaving virtually no temporal separation between independent interactions (so they may as well have happened simultaneously in direct contact with one another); this particularly applies to spin which supersedes all temporal effects as it operates independent of spatial (and then temporal) propagation. Deterministic "shrinking" is inherently a factor as well in that all possible outcomes are previously "acknowledged" before a particle separates physically from its counte

3.
Spectrum

The only real colors there are, are not colors at all: black and white. When admixed they make gray; but that is only for two dimensions. When a third extended dimension is introduced, they produce light and dark (for such concepts must act upon space to be manifest), and with the degrees of shade come the natural colors: yellow is light dimmed, blue is dark lightened, green is in between, and all the rest follow - serene. This observation is due to Goethe, though without physical elaboration.

So next time you look at colors, understand they are black (which requires no dimension), white (which requires two dimensions), and that all the colors of the rainbow are in glorious 3D.

4.
Ability
Versus
Will

Math is a language that is enchanting for its beauty. I would scarcely think there would not be a single instance of producing something out of abstraction if there were not some lack of capability on the part of an entire segment of the populace.

5.
Anthropic Selectivity

There are precisely three varieties of "selection" which account for life intelligent - and willing - enough to question the origin of its own existence (and they are also the answer): material selection, whereby planetary solar formations beget the geological and atmospheric properties necessary for the implantation of the seed of life; natural selection, whereby species are skimmed and whittled into suitable forms for increasing dominance of their environment; and social selection, whereby intellectual pursuits are valued and honored, and deemed worthy enough to "exist" as conceptual quandaries in the first place. In other words, in the end, and by our own "selection", we make the question - of the origin of our existence - and it is only relevant, and only even exists, insofar as we do.

6.
Updated Peter Principle

Joe Blow selection [the opposite of natural selection]: the tendency for a human population to favor underachievers due to unserendipitous conditions as well as the convenience of avoiding threats to a power structure which favors the lowest common denominator.

7.
Deep Blue

No machine, no matter how sophisticated, can ever "think". Thought is the eternal virtue man has above all other modes of existence, which is why humans will always be able to defeat any chess- playing machine.

8.
A Conversation on the Reductive Nature of Consciousness

"What are your views on Penrose's and Hameroff's Orchestrated Reduction of Quantum Coherence in
Brain Microtubules? I can see some validity to aspects of their theories..."

I think it's an accurate assessment. Human thought is necessarily non-computable, for Schopenhauer's reason that the *knower* remains *unknown* - for if their thought could ever be perceived, the perception would encompass it, and thus be part of it; which reduces only to actually *being* said knower – in addition to Gödel's theorem, as well as my deduction of the need for a unique reference frame for the appearance of consistent physical relations (i.e., a unique, non-universal consciousness); the observer, which begets the observed. Causal sequence is the unique linking factor from one moment to the next, so there cannot be a strict standard of measurement which determines the set of all that can occur in consciousness - this also being why time can exist at all, rather than being an aggregated, all- encompassing, self-contained unitary entity.

Additionally, Penrose's classification of existence into the three realms of physical, mental, and platonic is correct; this is what Descartes left out - rather than a dualism of mental/physical, there is a third tertiary linkage between them (mental/platonic/physical). The platonic is the world of potentiality, the mental is the world of actuality, and the physical is the world of determinism. The proper division order may be: platonic/mental/physical. Or physical/platonic/mental, or mental/physical/platonic, as long as they are in that order. From this we can infer that physics governs the physical, pure mathematics governs the platonic, and the mental governs itself in the image of the former two - that is because it makes its own rules, as the mirror of the Will, however the Will itself is the common intersection of physics and mathematics (the indivisible quantity-less, 0). With physics we can deduce the electrical-quantum aspects of brain functioning to produce the mind; from the platonic we can infer the universal Platonic Idea (in Schopenhauer's extended sense) which governs the classification of man's place (as a whole) in relation to Nature, in an almost Aristotelian way; and the mental provides the reference frame between the two, whose stability takes the form of "knowledge" of these in its own terms (as it makes its own rules).

The limit of the physical in its capacity to explain the mind as a feature of the brain can be inferred from the observed measurement of the time frame delimiting conscious functioning (500 milliseconds or half a second). The mind, as an electrical byproduct of the brain, can be inferred to be merely the sum electrical discharge in neuronal microtubules all having a common intersection of functioning and consistency of activity building up to an alteration in chemical structure for a period of exactly such one half a second.

All of this forms the fundamental basis for the physical aspect of mental activity (the most interesting scientific perspective), but it doesn't end there; consciousness is clearly, in a self-evident way, and in a way which serves as the only binding element for its phenomenon, logically sequential,

continuous; but clearly electrical firing in synapses is discontinuous and discrete. Therefore the basis of consciousness must lie in an objective, constant reference frame which is receiving these electro-chemical impressions, alterations, permutations, within the spacetime surrounding their occurrence (which must also govern it)
- a "central" reference frame. This reference frame supersedes, yet perfectly coincides with, the system of operation for the cumulative organization of massive bodies as a self-referencing, closed unit. In our closed system, gravity's governance is king, determining cycling bodies to exist in a self-consistent, closed loop.

The central, chief governing element of this system is the sun, and the manifestation of its reference frame is the extended force of spatial displacement, electromagnetic radiation, most visibly, light. Sunlight is then the objective reference frame of the mind, with respect to the electrical discharges of the brain; it forms the "surface" upon which they make ripples. This works perfectly well as light is a constant. But again, more specifically it is EM radiation, which permeates every facet of the solar system. Even if the sun were to burn out, its bodily presence would still exude gravitational waves traveling at the speed of light, thus providing an equal base of reference. If the sun were to catastrophically disappear, the central governance would become the aggregate, at any given moment in time, of the cumulative contribution of a multi-body system. And the same gravity waves would be emitted in the proper governing formation.

So there you have it, the canvass for consciousness is just as important as the paint.

9.
What "=" Equals

Equivalence is a self-reinforcing, self-existent principle.*10. Intelligentsia*

The definition of intelligence: the level of capability to distinguish between the specialized and generalized.

11.
The Scope of Scientific Observation

Philosophy: Properly, the science of concepts.

V
Philosophy

1.
On the Categorical Imperative

To say that doing what everyone should be doing is a good idea is optimal for a society made up of everyone.

2.
The 10 Most Important Philosophical Concepts of All Time

10. The mechanical universe and perception as the basis of knowledge. (Descartes)

9. The categorical imperative as well as distinction of phenomenon and noumenon. (Kant)

8. Laying the conceptual foundation of the Democratic Republic. (Locke)

7. The hermeneutic circle of Being. (Heidegger)

6. The hedonic calculus of utilitarianism. (Mill)

5. The nothingness condition of consciousness. (Sartre)

4. The origination of the Form (or Idea), which lays the foundation for the geometric mathematical universe. (Plato)

3. The logical reduction of atomic propositions. (Wittgenstein)

2. The identity of organic motive as the Will to Power. (Nietzsche)

1. The identification of the noumenon as Will. (Schopenhauer)

*3.
First
Law*

What is the deepest possible philosophical insight? Perception that the whole is NOT greater than the sum of its parts. This is the greatest possible insight, (1), because it entails ALL, as a WHOLE; (2), because it includes all possible details of its contributive constitution in one fell swoop. Recognition that they are ONE and the same entity is the greatest mathematical truth, the highest philosophical recognition, and the bane of all senseless speculation.

From this we may infer that the universe is whole, and constant, by definition; and that its physical parts comprise all that may possibly exist within it, always - this leaves no place for a beginning or an end (the greater universe at large may be regarded as a multiverse with unlimited mini-"universes" composing it).

From the grandest insight we may also infer that mind as a whole is not distinct from the physical components comprising it - and everything else - and that in order for qualia to arise abstractly this means that mind must be a mathematical synonymy of all its composite electrochemical activity - a synchronous correlative average which "syncs up" to the present moment.

Finally, we may confirm that there is an absolute truth - and it is the condition of truth-hood itself, WHOLLY - and all composite truths which contribute to its larger picture are verifiable facts, which cannot be questioned - in contrast to arbitrary or willful perceptions (i.e., wishful thinking).

4.
Why

Philosophy exists for lack of anything better to do. And it persists because people don't know enough, or enough about how to do it, or that it
has already been completed.

5.
Sounds Like

To resolve the tree falling in a forest dispute once and for all . . . all of it is contingent on the definition of "sound", which, contrary to the realization of most, requires MEMORY. "That 'sounds' like . . ."; sound is a resemblance, a memory (and interpretation) of innate capacities for cognition, in accordance with the
capacity for imagination of strict Platonic Ideals as sheer potentialities - for example this means that
musical notes can be conceived internally even by one who was born deaf, due to their structural relations

of harmony with one another (no note is an island - or frequency for that matter). They "link" themselves
into consciousness by virtue of their continuum. This is how "being" comes into being.

6.
*Past
Master*

Bertrand Russell echoes the hollowest and most inanely self-evident of platitudes. They are sheer tautology.

7.
Secrets Don't Make Friends

The "conspiracy of silence." Schopenhauer coined the term in reference to the first scholastic response to his works - or lack thereof. Nietzsche later laid the groundwork in explaining why this would occur: it is a rare kind of man that goes against the herd, paves his own path out of blood and iron, and traverses the road not traveled. It is only natural then for the sheep (or caribou, if you prefer) to vigorously avoid participating in, and thereby promoting, an intellectual framework which is their very own undoing.

This is what happens every time a great truth is pointed towards.

8.
Reciprocity

Philosophy is reciprocally inversive to religion.

9.
Dismissal from Ignorance

Philosophy arose as an effort to question and quell the necessity of sufferings, illfare, and the general problems of life where no other mode of thought, speculation, or science could. It addressed the question of existence, namely human existence, itself as a baseline. Some philosophers have been successful in this pursuit, whereas others have only perturbed the discipline.

Not recognizing the relevance of philosophical thought as a necessity for human life, as a means of dealing with its shortcomings, is either a privilege for those with the relatively unique condition of health and wealth, or a characteristic of a disprivileged cretin who cannot think enough to acknowledge the inherently woesome nature of existence.

10.
God

I will admit that God exists; in the sense of Schopenhauer's Will. It is an inextricable conclusion that the Will exists for the general case in the driving scheme of Nature, and that this Will can be coherently manipulated by our actions - in rearranging the order of our existence, we can bring about outcomes which are favored by the providence and precision of the execution of our design. It may be called "magic", or even sorcery, but it is actually the arrangement of all the infinitude of possible measurements to bring about the one that coincides with the timeline of our own consciousness - the greater encompassing timeline which encompasses our own is the intellect of God. But this God is inseparable from the mechanical, though he has in addition to distant manifestations a personal influence, and is ultimately a property of our position of awareness within the inclusive scheme of Nature; a reflection of us, in other words, like a bird flying over a pond, or ourselves in a mirror.

11.
Threshold

There is a limit to how far sophistry and reverse psychology can go . . . I think we're living in an
age which proves this.

12.
Deep
Sleep

The soundest rest and comfort that one can have can only follow from the solid knowledge and highest wisdom that, as certain as any law of physics, idiocy is, in the end, ultimately self-defeating.

VI
Interpretation

1.
Proof

Everything that exists can be proven. The question is whether or not one accepts, comprehends, or is capable of fathoming the means of such proof.

2.

Preparedness

Would the average person recognize, understand, or know how to properly respond to the absolute truth if he was confronted by it, face to face? Or would he be as a deer in headlights, unable to fathom his next step? He would certainly not be in any position to spread his revelation to others, or even utter so much as the slightest acknowledgement of his discovery. So it is here with countless unknowns who scurry and cower from timeless, time-tested epiphany after epiphany that is revealed. It is no discredit to the light- bearer that they have not bowed in reverence, merely a to-be-expected consequence of their inherent impotence in the face of such light.

3.
Moral of the Story

Jurassic Park is like a better version of Frankenstein. They address the very same theme, bringing life to the lifeless (or extinct), and have the same moral - what can be done does not equate to what should be done; particularly with a scientific bent. Or perhaps it all goes back to the fruit of knowledge (of good and evil) in the Garden of Eden. Jurassic Park still trumps them. It is, needless to say, more realistic than the

Eden fable, incorporating evolutionary genesis and extinction directly, and superior to Frankenstein's nightmarish fantasy of resurrecting a single being from the dead - in this a plethora of myriad species is reborn, and wreak much more havoc and thus impress upon the imagination a much more stringent message. It is much more appealing to one's curiosity, to mass-marketing interests, and to one's sense of intricate [science] fiction.

At the very least, these three fables are a sign of their respective times - Eden for primitive man, bereft of technological understanding or capability (then it was a "God" and a "Tree"); reactivated neural tissue in the steampunk archaism of Mary

Shelley's masterwork (in reference to the writings of Charles's grandfather, Erasmus Darwin); and now the full-scale metaphor for not allowing organically-oriented technology to hastily overrun itself and make obsolete the initial purpose. Jurassic Park may be the most sophisticated morality tale to ever catch hold of the public's periphery then in this case . . . after all, aren't all stories' morals an anathema of evil, which in the end is a misuse of power, the root of which is knowledge? And is this not, being the age of unrivaled and exponential technological progress, the most critical time for this message?

4.
Monk Dictator

Every moment of perception is a simultaneous union of ignorance and enlightenment. At once every relevant piece of information may be apprehended by the intellect, and one may also be completely as they were as a child, when every image, every vision, was so new, so unique, so fresh . . . unmarred by acquired contention and thought process. Is it really the case that knowing everything can really be like knowing nothing? In other words, can knowledge become so overwhelming and over-rich that it leaves one hopelessly confounded in the mystery of its genesis? Or is the ignorance of a child the greatest wisdom?

5.
Classic Distinction

What, if any, is the difference between classical music and modern rock? I have found it to be the case that the vast majority of modern rock musicians have great difficulty in composing decent work. Whereas classical musicians compose works of great genius quite regularly. Why is that? One would think that the greater complexity of the classical genre would make it more difficult to create decent work, but this does not seem to be the case. Is a core melody then so incomprehensibly unfathomable to produce? Or are most humans simply totally inept when it comes to harmony even on the most rudimentary level?

6.
Nature
Versus
Nurture

Half of all truly great work (be it artistic, scientific, or logical) is an accident. This is a statistical law which results from the fact that the Will only makes up precisely one half of any endeavor, and its representation (Nature - here, Chance) makes up the other half. To make the best of work, one must not only have genius but luck and serendipity on one's side.

7.
Name Calling

All of language originated as, and is ultimately a means of, identification of phenomena, most centrally, of the self - in the form of naming. People tend to forget that words ultimately have no meaning beyond what we ascribe to them at a given fleeting instant, and disappear just as quickly as they arose to our processing. So it is with all the phenomena themselves; they don't exist long enough to say that they exist, in any objective and meaningful sense. This is why substance is no mystery, as THERE IS NOTHING THERE TO BE MYSTERIOUS.

8.
Entreaty

Do you not think that the universe is at least as complex, and more so, perhaps infinitely more, than the brain it contains? Aren't the rhythms, the ebbs and flows of life far too subtle to be grasped even with the most strenuous effort? What makes you think that life should be so readily explained then, most particularly, the course of its evolution? Just because life forms seem too complex to have come from nowhere doesn't mean that they did, or had to. Interesting that you claim that a magical being had to produce them, which is tantamount to indeed saying they really came out of nowhere - as opposed to being an intrinsic time-trialed product of the universe's innate ebb and flow . . .

9.
Semantics

The point at which a discussion shifts to semantics is precisely the point at which it has lost all meaning.

10.
The
Nature of
Music

Music is never just a collection of sounds; it is not merely the preferred language of the expression of the spirit - as its harmonies being fractions of octaves are sheer temporal congruences which emulate conscious experience (as that which is also measured by time) - it is not even merely the quintessential commemorative edifice, forever erecting spaceless monuments to eternity which ennoble and crystallize human aspirations and achievement . . . nay, it is the very spoken word of the mouth of God . . . and its limitless possibilities are what define His parameters.

11.
Mind-Reader

To imply that you know woman's veracity is to imply that you can read other people's minds - a classic superstitious childhood delusion. Woman is a mystery, who has every reason to be false towards, and the enemy of, her biological opposite - man. And acts as such in every available instance.

12. The Importance of Trust

Where there is no trust, there can be no love.

13. Plane of Sight

The universe is really only a reflection of our way of looking at it.

14. Knowledge

The truth doesn't need to be acknowledged. It knows itself.

15.
Falsehood

The white lie is the flourish of the imbecile.

16.
Art

Art is: evidence of perfected action.

17.
Centrifugal Force

When traveling in a circle, moving backwards makes just as much progress as moving forward.

18.
Misery
Loves
Company

Why is it that when you're miserable time seems to last forever, but when you're happy it seems to vanish? It is because misery is more true to reality, that is, more real. And thus there is more of it to experience.

19.
The Root of Evil

The only truly evil thing is the concept of the evil itself.

20.
Sounding Board

Not only do our minds reflect the physical world, but likewise, the physical world reflects our minds - in the general unity of the scheme of things.

21.
Genius

What really defines genius is complete unpredictability with the inter-stitched substitute appearance of plausible alternatives.

22.
Malice

Malice is indistinguishable from stupidity, and vice-versa.

23.
Creation

Art is about transcending limitations and creating something permanent out of a state of flux.

24.
Assumption

Unfit generalizations can only follow from a general unfitness.

25.
Ex Nihilo

Not understanding how existence comes into being is no different than not understanding how 1 plus 1 equals 2. 1 is the same as itself, thus it implies itself - again. 2 follows naturally hence; more thus comes from less - and something, thus from nothing.

26.
Astral Projection

Music is nothing less than the language of the heavens, made sensible.

27.
Failure of Communication

Is there a more posing conundrum than trying to convince someone that they don't actually know better
- exactly when they don't know enough, even to know it?

28.
Motive

The instinct for non-reactionary derision always proceeds from a feeling of incompetence.

29.
Error

Hypocrisy and logical inconsistency are the same; lack of recognizing this from the start is the source of all necessary failure in the end.

30.
Field of Vision

Many tend to forget that they can only see the world as well as their minds will let them, and that what they see can only appear in terms of their own abilities . . . and some have even forgotten to take the lens cap off. It is little wonder then that so many gratefully indulge in such a blissful, though understandably temporary, amnesia.

31.
Poetic Justice

The greatest conceivable crime with the surest and most immediate form of natural punishment:

the possession of a falsely earned sense of ego - without even having the potential to realize it.

32.
Hilarity

They say human life is a divine comedy; and it is. But somehow I'm not laughing.

33.
Youth and Age

There is no greater gulf in existence than the chasm which separates knowledge and wisdom.

34.
Subtlety

Effortlessness and mindlessness . . . a subtle distinction, the ability to make which separates higher life from lower.

35.
Masterwork

Those who cannot create are condemned to destroy; for they cannot stand to be in a lively world whose very existence is a constant mockery of their own incompetence, a mirror reflecting their inability to mirror it. Destruction is their only masterpiece; flaw and failure, their only finished work.

36.
Value

The sole objective measure of a man's intrinsic value and worth lies in his capacity to appreciate
and understand geometry.

37.
Meaning

Infinite, endless, with no beginning: what do these mean? They mean that past, present, and future, are one; a timeless void echoing a single vision of unity - the future already happened long ago, was written long before it could have ever been realized. All is merely a play, a dancing light show in the shadows, in wait for us to realize this; and this is the ONE great realization that can ever occur, the point at which all ends meet, and where the vast, endless, impersonal

Absolute becomes the sole, individual thought.

38.
Query

Every question has an answer - except the one that isn't asked.

39.
Strength in Numbers

There is no weaker an ally than a lie.

40.
The Mysterious

Why is the mysterious the most beautiful thing that we can experience? Because only the mysterious holds out the promise of new life - nor can the unknown, the unrevealed, hurt us; it can only afford us, through disinterested observation, renewed interest and intrigue . . . in what lay before us the entire time.

41.
The
Chosen

In the world as it stands today, ignorance is the truest virtue - for if the light of knowledge were to shine in all its scorching radiance upon all, it would soon become very clear that only the smallest minority, which happened to also share in it and thus were able to reflect it back,
would be left to stand.

VII
Life

1.
Tit for Tat

If you're going to be mind-bogglingly stupid, I'm going to be mind-bogglingly crazy. This is the natural response, is it not?

2.
Worship

Let us worship the imagination, not the image. Let us celebrate genius above all else, as that glorious portal to eternal, infinite youth, in the most unexpected of places. Let us acknowledge that a Deity's power can never be greater than our potential reverence for It. If this is done, we would be lifting humanity to the properly noble heights among the galaxy's finest, where he may assume his true place . .. among the stars.

3.
Desire

I shall be so bold to say that any desire so deep that it reaches to the very core of a man can be attained. That is because his core is in line with the mechanics of the universe. At least, with adequate technological faculties at his disposal, as such a potential success rate requires as much efficiency from the machinery of Nature/Man as possible. But at any rate, desires are based entirely upon living potentials, which by nature, can happen.

4.
Loss

When you lose someone, you never really lose them. That part of the universe which had the capacity to encompass them remains, as an ever-ready reminder in the endlessly recurrent theme of existence.

5.
Fame

All anyone wants is attention. Male, female; black, white; rich, poor. This is the root desire which stems from the need for one's needs to be attended to; attention - that is, accommodation become conscious - is the most specific form of attendance to one's physical well-being, the sum drive of purpose itself; part and parcel.

This is what motivates art; this is what motivates science. It is not merely fame, for fame can entail infamy, and complete disregard for one's well-being. No, it is more than this - complete, unadulterated, utterly undifferentiated "attention". This subsumes and supersedes the will to power, as power is utterly useless without attention.

6.
Insanity

Happiness is a state of living insanity. That is the only conceivable way one can be "happy" in a world as this.

7.
Sex

What is the origin of sexual desire? Why do I have attraction towards women? Do women have sexual desire? What is the mechanism behind this phenomenon.

I suppose I must attempt to address .

It stems entirely from the male genitalia, and is an effort to find a "host" who appears the most accommodating intrinsically - and by virtue of comparison, the male counterpart is excluded. This is why women appear "softer" and "gentler"; more "accommodating". And bam! $1 + 2 = 3$. A light goes on. Off? Odd that they mean the same thing . . . but I digress.

Where was I? Ah, yes. Woman seems accommodating to the male genitalia in the same way a piece of fruit is accommodating to the tongue. Nothing more. We'd engage in coitus with robots if they looked accommodating enough; hyper-intelligent, humanoid chimpanzees if they could speak enough to talk dirty to us. The man is intrinsically geared towards accommodating his own genitalia in the same way a light bulb is accommodated by screwing it into a socket.

So do women experience sexual desire? I believe they only experience it insofar as they want to see their own bodies appreciated for being what they perceive as "hot", and "sexual". I believe they are in it entirely for themselves, to vicariously experience self-actualization, not to consume a desirable, complementary other half, as males do.

8.
What A Woman Wants

Since sexual exchange between consenting adults is inherently an economic enterprise by virtue of the supply and demand laws which govern its generative qualities, women themselves as progenitors of procreation, when dating, are not seeking rock hard abs, a sturdy member, an attractive partner, a loving relationship, fruitful progeny, or - this one's my favorite - *humor*; they are seeking, in short, nothing short of economic stability.

9.
Ancient Funerary Inscription

"At the doorway to darkness; cut down by lightning coming from the stars."

10.
Female Intuition

If woman was of equal intelligence to man, she would be in a miserable condition indeed. She must be equal parts greater and lesser in that respect, both to lack the common sense to avoid him, and to possess the cunning to manipulate him.

11. Purpose

Philosophy is for the lost. Religion is for the damned.

12. Adversity

Strength can only be developed through adversity.

13.
Death

I believe that the moment of death entails an immediate and continuous vision of entrance into the very next life, the next birth. There is no disconnection. There is no turning off. There is only reawakening. The body goes to sleep, but the mind reaches for the light and rises.

14.
Sexuality

The feminine is inherently sexual; the masculine is not.

15.
Mission

To vanish into surreality before a blaze of undying glory - that is the highest mission and code of life.

16.
Gender Roles

The role of the masculine is that of a death-enforcer whose business is life. The role of the feminine is that of a life-enforcer whose business is death.

17.
Justice

The more undignifying the injustice, the more proliferously it sows the seeds of its own undoing, the more it unravels its own web, the more mercilessly it heaves itself onto its own sword of self-defeat. For justice and logic are unified, and no contravention of the rights of man is long-lived when facing the dawn of the judgment of Nature; That which disperses the archaic hypotheses of old to the wind, ever irrevocably.

18. Eternity

Nobody needs eternal life. A single moment can stretch out to infinity.

19.
Adoration

Women love men for what they do. Men love women for who they are.

20.
Pearls Before Swine

All geniuses are tortured . . . if only by the mediocrity around them. Only hopeless suffering can push the mind to its limits and dispel all hopeful assumptions about the world - unshrouding the blanket of false optimism to reveal the precipice leading to the abyss: the infinite.

21.
Mirror

We never truly experience the best in life until we are faced with extreme adversity; it crystallizes and reflects the best in us - as it is a mirror.

22.
Sentience

Where would we be without idiots? They teach us what not to do, and implicitly give away the key to their own undoing as well in the process.

23.
Apish

Lack of intellect is chiefly compensated for in the physical realm; and when all else fails, there is no other resort but brute force.

24.
Tao

The lesson of all lessons? Consciousness rules the conscious world; not the mindless whims of the numberless ignorant leches who leech off the inheritance it so readily provides, without which they would be consigned to their proper role as the immanent prey of the jungle they so amply worship.

25.
Time

Over and done before it's begun ~ the greatest of riddles under the sun.

26.
Power

True power isn't something that can be found, or acquired; it IS, an effortless intrinsic quality of the powerful. All others must contradict logic in their efforts to squeeze it from the fruits of the tree of nature.

27.
True Sin

The sum of all sin proceeds from the pretense of being more than one is.

28.
Affluence

The degree to which a man craves wealth is in precise inverse proportion to his natural vitality and stake in life itself.

29.
Comedy

Humor is often a measure of one's awareness. If one can't appreciate the sublime inanity and ludicrous enterprise that is human existence at this period of time and come away with a boisterous laugh every now and again as it rears its head in plain sight, one has to be either the actual clown of mockery in question, or a suicidally disaffected melancholiac.

30. Black Sheep

Even the slightest display of thinking capacity is decried by the thoughtless as the most heinous form of villainy; no less than a mortal antagonist to them and their ilk - of course, this being due to the necessary destruction of the cloud ignorance it entails, a cloud which was all that shrouded them and thus sustained their livelihood to begin with.

31.
Maxim for the New Age

I hate Man, but love men. I hate women, but love Woman. Can you tell me why?

32.
Ever Knower

Where is the last birthed moment gone? And from whence shall the next dead arrive? To the unseeing eye, the answer, unknown - but to the all-seeing they were never alive.

33.
Epilogue

Into the dark, the great beyond . . .
Nothing of which I could be more fond,
Than to sprawl into the cavernous reach
Of ill-grasped depths, which yonder, beseech . . .

After-Words
(On Logical Fallacy)

Seated within one man is the character of all mankind; and just one man is capable of speaking for all men. Let his actual words be the judge of such a standard to which he is held.

Not understanding axiomatic or philosophical fact is no different from not grasping a mathematical theorem. Its truth is beyond dispute, and remains factual whether or not one wants it to be.

Ad hominem is not always fallacious, particularly when the other arguer is exhibiting "ad idiotum". Nor is circular logic always, when truth itself is a self-confirming circle.

Those who wish to argue for argument's sake will never acknowledge the final conclusion, for they wish to continue arguing.

The "fallacy fallacy" is that by which an accuser finds fault in the faultless. The means by which an attacker finds vulnerability in the invulnerable. Just because they claim to have discovered such gaps in the defenses of others does not mean they successfully have; and ultimately only exposes their own defenselessness.

All roads converge to a polar vertex in the end.

"Silent enim leges inter arma."

Table of Content :

Arthur Schopenhauer (19th Century)
p. 4

Friedrich Nietzsche (19th Century)
p. 8

Me
p. 9

Statement of Purpose
(In Other Words)
p. 11

I - Being
p.13

I I - Religion
p. 28

III - Society
p. 44

IV - Science
p. 56

V - Philosophy
p. 77

VI - Interpretation
p. 92

VII - Life
p. 123

After-Words (On Logical Fallacies)
p. 128

blank page

Contino Publishers Ltd.
Dorking, Uk

www.ingramcontent.com/pod-product-compliance
Lightning Source LLC
Chambersburg PA
CBHW071509040426
42444CB00008B/1562